WITHDRAWN

Marion Public Library
1101 6th Ave
Marion, IA 52302
(319) 377-3412

WHO WE ARE

THE NATIVE AMERICAN EXPERIENCE

Stuart A. Kallen

San Diego, CA

About the Author

Stuart A. Kallen is the author of more than 350 nonfiction books for children and young adults. He has written on topics ranging from the theory of relativity to the art of electronic dance music. In 2018 Kallen won a Green Earth Book Award from the Nature Generation environmental organization for his book *Trashing the Planet: Examining the Global Garbage Glut*. In his spare time he is a singer, songwriter, and guitarist in San Diego.

© 2023 ReferencePoint Press, Inc.
Printed in the United States

For more information, contact:
ReferencePoint Press, Inc.
PO Box 27779
San Diego, CA 92198
www.ReferencePointPress.com

ALL RIGHTS RESERVED.
No part of this work covered by the copyright hereon may be reproduced or used in any form or by any means—graphic, electronic, or mechanical, including photocopying, recording, taping, web distribution, or information storage retrieval systems—without the written permission of the publisher.

LIBRARY OF CONGRESS CATALOGING-IN-PUBLICATION DATA

Names: Kallen, Stuart A., 1955- author.
Title: The Native American experience / by Stuart A. Kallen.
Description: San Diego, CA : ReferencePoint Press, Inc., 2023. | Series: Who we are | Includes bibliographical references and index.
Identifiers: LCCN 2022027787 | ISBN 9781678204723 (library binding) | ISBN 9781678204730 (ebook)
Subjects: LCSH: Indians, Treatment of--United States--Juvenile literature. | Indians of North America--Government relations--Juvenile literature. | Indians of North America--Social conditions--Juvenile literature.
Classification: LCC E93 .K225 2023 | DDC 305.897/073--dc23/eng/20220629
LC record available at https://lccn.loc.gov/2022027787

CONTENTS

Native Americans: By the Numbers	4
Introduction Unique Cultures, Diverse People	6
Chapter One Early Life in America	10
Chapter Two Rebuilding Communities	20
Chapter Three Reclaiming Identity	29
Chapter Four Striving for Rights	38
Chapter Five Confronting Challenges	48
Source Notes	57
For Further Research	60
Index	62
Picture Credits	64

NATIVE AMERICANS: BY THE NUMBERS

Total Population
- 3.7 million identify as Native American or Alaska Native alone
- 5.9 million identify as Native American or Alaska Native in combination with another ethnic group

Youth Population
- 1.6 million Native American and Alaska Native young people under the age of 18

Number of Federally Recognized Tribes
- 574

Ten States with Largest American Indian/Alaska Native Populations

Largest Native American Tribe
- Navajo (Diné) Nation: population 399,494

Largest Reservation
- Navajo (Diné) Nation: 24,425 sq mi

Education

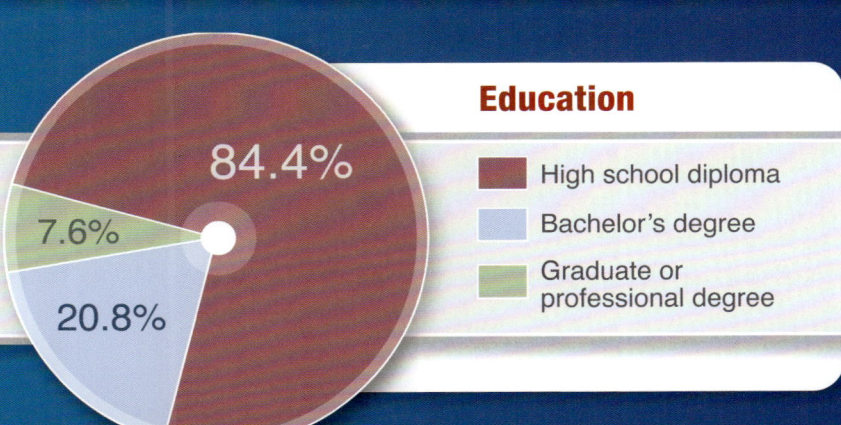

- 84.4% High school diploma
- 20.8% Bachelor's degree
- 7.6% Graduate or professional degree

Life Expectancy

For both men and women	78.4 years
For women	81.1 years
For men	75.8 years

INTRODUCTION

Unique Cultures, Diverse People

Native Americans have been part of American mythology for centuries. Since the first Europeans arrived in the 1500s, the country's indigenous people have been stereotyped in stories and works of art. White culture has depicted Native Americans in countless demeaning ways, portraying them alternately as noble warriors and Indian princesses or as brutal savages. Native American names and imagery have been used on American money, military attack helicopters, and toys; in advertisements; and as sports mascots. Many of these portrayals represent Native Americans as a single culture or people. Kevin Gover, who is a citizen of the Pawnee Tribe and director of the Smithsonian's National Museum of the American Indian, explains how these stereotypes took hold: "It was Hollywood that established our monolithic modern vision of American Indians, in blockbuster westerns . . . that depict all Indians, all the time, as horse-riding; tipi-dwelling; bow-, arrow- and rifle-wielding; buckskin-, feather- and fringe-wearing warriors."[1]

These stereotypes mask the reality of tribal nations that work every day to preserve a wide range of cultures, languages, and customs. In the 2020 census, 3.7 million people identified as Native American or Alaska Native, and 5.9 million people identified as Native American or Alaska Native in combination with another ethnic group. These indigenous Americans belong to 574 federally recognized Indian tribes—also called bands, pueblos, and Native villages. These nations have tribal sovereignty, the legal authority to govern themselves.

Census figures show that about 30 percent of Native Americans live in what is called Indian country, a term that defines all lands within the 318 Indian reservations located in 35 states. The remaining 70 percent of Native Americans live in towns, cities, suburbs, and rural areas all across America. Some call themselves Native Americans. Others prefer American Indians, Indians, or indigenous Americans. Many express their roots by referring to their nation's name in their own language, such as Diné (Navajo) or Tsalagi (Cherokee).

> "[Hollywood has long depicted] all Indians . . . as horse-riding; tipi-dwelling; bow-, arrow- and rifle-wielding; buckskin-, feather- and fringe-wearing warriors."[1]
>
> —Kevin Gover, director of the National Museum of the American Indian

Vibrant and Thriving

While Native Americans are often viewed through a lens of nostalgia as part of America's vanishing past, they remain a vibrant part of today's culture. In 2022 Native Americans were making the news in media, politics, the arts, and activism. Deb Haaland of the Pueblo of Laguna in New Mexico was chosen by President Joe Biden to be US secretary of the interior, the first Native American to serve in a president's cabinet. On television *Reservation Dogs*, cocreated by Seminole filmmaker Sterlin Harjo, is the first show created with an entirely indigenous cast and production team. Young Native American environmental activists like Jasilyn Charger and Xiuhtezcatl Martinez are fighting to protect the environment from oil drilling and climate change. In the world of art, the works of esteemed Salish painter Jaune Quick-to-See Smith can be viewed in prestigious museums, including the Whitney Museum of American Art in New York City and the National Gallery of Art in Washington, DC. Seneca sculptor Marie Watt and other indigenous artists are presenting Native American views and voices at major exhibitions in museums across the country.

These luminaries and others are serving as warriors for their communities, as Robert Martin, president of the Institute of American Indian Arts, explains: "Indigenous warriors are cultural and spiritual leaders who are responsible for protecting the land,

The television series Reservation Dogs is the first show with an entirely indigenous cast and production team.

health, and welfare of each community member. . . . Traditional tribal leadership manifests qualities reflected in the 'servant leadership' model . . . [that] focuses on one's service to the community and the creation of an environment where everyone can realize their full potential."[2]

Rising Up and Pushing Back

The desire to nurture and maintain a rich cultural and spiritual heritage is something that unites many Native Americans, wherever they live. But the struggle has been long and difficult. Old World diseases like smallpox, measles, and scarlet fever devastated indigenous societies beginning in the seventeenth century. Those who survived faced forced removal from their lands and a government campaign of genocide. These efforts are reflected in the words of General William T. Sherman. After a fierce battle between the US Army and the Lakota Sioux in South Dakota in 1866, Sherman wrote, "We must act with vindictive earnestness against the Sioux, even to their extermination, of men, women, and children. . . . During an assault the soldiers can not pause to distinguish between male and female, or even discriminate as to age."[3]

The campaign to exterminate Native Americans failed, although this and other government actions helped create conditions of extreme poverty among America's indigenous populations. Many Native Americans struggled to overcome poverty and discrimination. By the 1960s activists had started pushing back against both.

By the 1980s some tribes had found a way to bring much-needed income, jobs, and prosperity to the reservations. They built casinos that attracted both recreational and serious gamblers from around the nation. By 2015 around half of all federally recognized tribes were managing gaming operations worth around $25 billion annually. While this money does benefit the Native American nations that run casinos, 58 percent do not have gaming operations because they live in extremely isolated areas. Those who live on rural reservations are the most impoverished people in the United States. Their health is disproportionately worse than any other group, and life on these reservations is marred by substance abuse, violence, and suicide.

Centuries of land theft, forced relocation, and cultural destruction have taken a toll on Native American communities, but many continue to reclaim their identities and determine their own fates. And tribal histories are still being written in indigenous languages, including Diné, Mohawk, Kiowa, Inuit, and Hopi.

The Native American story is as diverse and unique as each individual and as powerful as a common community connected by adversity, wisdom, spirituality, and destiny. Indigenous people are working to reconnect to their roots, counter stereotypes, and highlight the important contributions made by the nation's original inhabitants.

CHAPTER ONE

Early Life in America

American schoolchildren have long been taught about a period called the age of discovery. This era from the fifteenth through eighteenth centuries was a time when the English, French, Spanish, and other European explorers sailed to North America and built settlements. Some old history books make it sound as if the explorers had discovered a vacant land. In 1987 a widely used high school textbook called *American History: A Survey* reinforced this idea: "For thousands of centuries . . . in which human races were evolving, forming communities, and building the beginnings of national civilizations in Africa, Asia, and Europe—the continents we know as the Americas stood empty of mankind and its works." The book goes on to state that Europeans created "a civilization where none existed."[4]

Despite the notion that North America was an untouched wilderness, anthropologists estimate that before the fifteenth century around 10 million indigenous people lived in what is now the United States. They spoke over three hundred languages, according to the Indigenous Language Institute. While early European colonists called the land the New World, it was an ancient expanse of earth that had been shaped by Native Americans for more than ten thousand years. Around two thousand years ago, the Hohokam people of Arizona built a series of dams and more than 500 miles (805 km) of canals to provide water to approximately fifty thousand people. On the West Coast the Mono, Karuk, and Yurok people burned the underbrush that surrounded ancient sequoia and redwood trees to attract game animals and prevent large, destructive wildfires. And almost everywhere freshwater flowed, Native

Americans lined river banks with basket traps to catch fish. Ancient archaeological records show that tribes traded seeds, food, animal skins, precious stones, and other goods with one another through a system of interconnected trails that linked thousands of villages across the continent.

Nations of the Northeast

Before the arrival of Europeans, Native Americans did not have guns, horses, livestock, metal tools, or vehicles with wheels. However, their hunting, fishing, and agricultural skills allowed them to enjoy an exceptionally varied diet in a fertile land that teemed with plants and animals. This helped Native American communities thrive in almost every part of North America.

Indigenous people had many different governing systems, cultural traditions, languages, and spiritual practices. However, there were some similarities. Most Native American groups were made up of extended families, or clans. Clans held a special place in Native American life as explained by Jake Aguonia and other tribal elders of the Anishinaabe people of the Great Lakes region: "Your clan is with you from the day you are born. It is said that your clan walks with you and looks after you. Your clan takes care of you so that you don't have to go through life without help and protection."[5]

Some of the clans—though related—lived far apart, went by different names, and spoke different dialects of the same language. The Haudenosaunee Confederacy is an example of distant but related clans. The confederacy, also known as the Six Nations of the Iroquois, originally included the Mohawk, Oneida, Tuscarora, Onondaga, Cayuga, and Seneca peoples. They spoke different Iroquoian dialects. They occupied thousands of villages spanning hunting grounds and farmland in present-day New York and Pennsylvania and around the eastern Great Lakes region all the way up into parts of southern Canada.

Haudenosaunee translates as "People of the Longhouse." Longhouses were large shelters constructed from layers of birch bark over wooden poles. They could be up to 250 feet (76 m) long

This map shows the major Native American cultural regions in North America as they were when the Europeans first arrived. It also names some of the tribes living in each region.

and 25 feet (7.6 m) wide. Twenty or more families might share a longhouse. The Haudenosaunee cultivated corn, beans, and squash—crops they referred to as the Three Sisters. Early French explorers noted that 6 square miles (15.5 sq. km) of cornfields surrounded each Haudenosaunee village.

Native Americans who lived in present-day New England were part of the Wampanoag tribal confederation, which included the Patuxet, Mashpee, and Nantucket peoples. These clans spoke dialects of the Algonquian language, which was also spoken by nations as varied as the Delaware Lenapé, the Ojibwa in the upper Midwest, and the Blackfoot of the Great Plains. As with many other Native Americans throughout the continent, corn provided a nutritional staple that allowed the Wampanoag to thrive. English explorer John Smith expressed his amazement at the bountiful landscape shaped by the Patuxet in present-day Massachusetts. In his 1616 book *A Description of New England*, Smith wrote that the land is "so planted with Gardens and Corne fields, and so well inhabited with a goodly, strong and well proportioned people . . . [that] I would rather live here than any where."[6]

Great Plains and Western Nations

In the central part of North America, vast prairies covered the land between the Mississippi River and the Rocky Mountains. An estimated 50 million bison (often called buffalo) occupied these grasslands. Bison provided food, clothing, and shelter to dozens of Native American nations, including the Ojibwa, Lakota, Pawnee, Kiowa, and Cheyenne.

People of the Great Plains considered the bison as both a sacred animal and a provider of all necessities. The meat was roasted, dried, or made into soup. Bison hides were fashioned into clothing, drums, and other items. Large hides were sewn together to create cone-shaped shelters called tepees.

In the Pacific Northwest more than one hundred Native American nations prospered along the coast from California to Alaska. This cool, rainy region was home to communities including the Tlingit in the north and the Salish, Pomo, and Yurok further south. The coastal regions teemed with seals, walruses, whales, oysters, lobsters, and other seafood. Salmon and other fish were abundant in pristine mountain rivers that flowed cold and clear from the Sierra Nevada range. Historian Roxanne Dunbar-

Ortiz describes the people of the Pacific Northwest: "Great seafaring and fishing peoples flourished, linked by culture, common ceremonies, and extensive trade. These were wealthy peoples living in a comparative paradise of natural resources, including the sacred salmon. . . . They crafted gigantic wooden totems, masks, and lodges carved from giant sequoias and redwoods."[7]

> "Great seafaring and fishing peoples flourished [in the Pacific Northwest]. . . . These were wealthy peoples living in a comparative paradise of natural resources, including the sacred salmon."[7]
>
> —Roxanne Dunbar-Ortiz, historian

Indigenous people who lived between the Sierra Nevada and the Rocky Mountains did not have a paradise of natural resources. This region, known as the Great Basin, features an arid climate, brackish water, and high deserts that sizzle in the summer and freeze in the winter. But the Shoshone, Paiute, Ute, and Bannock, among others, understood the harsh rhythms of their environment. They fished and hunted rabbits, antelope, and waterfowl. In the summer they gathered pine nuts, roots, and tubers to store for cooking during the cold winter months.

The Southwestern Clans

In the rugged lands of the Southwest, the Navajo, Pueblo, Apache, and other indigenous peoples adapted to a dry landscape marked with mesas, canyons, mountains, and deserts. The Apache were nomadic people. Some clans followed migrating herds of bison while others set up temporary villages and planted crops. The Pueblo people built permanent adobe homes called pueblos. They cultivated corn, squash, and other crops and hunted small mammals like gophers and rabbits.

For more than eight thousand years, Native American women of the Southwest practiced the arts of basket weaving and pottery making. Baskets decorated with geometric patterns, flower themes, and animal images were used as backpacks, hats, and

Native Americans are depicted wearing wolf skins as they hunt bison (also known as buffalo). Before Europeans arrived with horses in the seventeenth century, nomadic communities hunted buffalo on foot, with bow and arrows.

utensils. Pottery bowls, jars, vases, and decorative items were emblazoned with intricately painted designs.

Blue-green turquoise stones were laboriously mined and painstakingly transformed into beads, bracelets, earrings, and necklaces with tools made from tortoise shells and elk horns. Turquoise served many functions. In addition to jewelry, the stone was infused with magical significance and was central to spiritual and healing rituals.

Spirits and Art

To the people of the Southwest—and to Native American clans throughout the continent—spirituality was central to daily life. While the religious practices of the clans were numerous, intricate, and different in each community, most held a central belief that the natural surroundings were permeated with spirits. All plants, animals, rocks, bodies of water, and weather phenomena were said to be governed by mystical life forces. These spirits could be helpful or harmful, depending on how they were treated. Native American spiritual practices revolved around praying to spirits, pondering their motives, and making offerings to appease them.

People of many nations, from the Ojibwa to the Haudenosaunee, also believed in a supreme being called the Great Spirit. This being was an ever-present active force without form who

The Haudenosaunee Confederacy

For centuries the five Iroquois-speaking clans in upstate New York were fierce rivals embroiled in constant conflict. According to Iroquois oral tradition, a wandering elder named Deganawida met up with Hiawatha, an Onondaga man, to unite the Mohawk, Oneida, Onondaga, Cayuga, and Seneca clans in the Haudenosaunee Confederacy. Anthropologists believe that this happened sometime around 1450. Deganawida and Hiawatha traveled to each of the five nations and presented the Great Law of Peace, which is the oral constitution of the Haudenosaunee Confederacy. The Great Law of Peace laid out about 115 decrees to unite the clans in symbolic kinship so they could live together in peace.

Leaders of the confederacy were selected by the most respected women in each clan. They elected fifty life-appointed sachems, or peace leaders, who represented the clans in a Grand Council. The council met whenever it needed to rule on disputes, represent the confederacy to outsiders, and coordinate group actions.

Framers of the US Constitution, including Benjamin Franklin and James Madison, studied the democratic ideals of the Haudenosaunee Confederacy. Some historians have suggested that the decrees of the Great Law of Peace were incorporated into the US Constitution, written in 1787.

oversaw all life on earth. In the mid-nineteenth century, anthropologist Lewis Henry Morgan befriended several Seneca leaders. Morgan explained his understanding of the Great Spirit in his 1851 book *The League of the Ho-dé-no-sau-nee or Iroquois*: "The Iroquois regarded the Great Spirit as the God of the Indian alone. . . . To him they rendered constant thanks and homage for the change of the seasons, the fruits of the earth, the preservation of their lives."[8]

In the wild lands of the subarctic the Yupik people of Alaska referred to their spirituality as the "Way of Life." This was based on the belief that animals could understand human speech and should be afforded the utmost respect. While obtaining food in a land of deep snow and frigid temperatures could be extremely challenging, hunters did not curse the animals no matter how great their hunger. Instead, they prayed to animal spirits and offered honor and devotion. After a successful hunt the Way of Life dictated that the animal be thanked for giving the gift of its life.

Wars and Warriors

Native Americans developed successful societies in North America from coast to coast for millennia. Like people everywhere, they also fought wars as a means of acquiring territory, controlling trade, and gaining respect and prestige. While there are no written accounts of war before Europeans arrived, oral histories often focus on battle and conquest. The Haudenosaunee, for example, were known as fierce warriors who engaged in battle with distant enemies and even neighboring clans. Attacks on a village would require the victims to take revenge. The wronged clans would capture prisoners, including women and children, to compensate for a loss.

Native Americans rarely conducted scorched earth warfare, in which enemy villages were burned to the ground and all men, women, and children were killed. This was a technique perfected by Europeans, who fought with organized armies, powerful weapons, and ruthless efficiency. Europeans were not interested in avenging wrongs or gaining respect. The explorers that began arriving in waves during the mid-1600s were looking for gold, which was not initially found in any great quantities. By the 1700s some Europeans were getting rich stripping the forests of fur-bearing animals, which were turned into fashionable clothes and hats for wealthy people in London, Paris, and elsewhere.

The fur trade had a serious impact on Native Americans. Traders carried common European diseases like smallpox, measles,

A series of battles known at the Sioux Wars, between the US Army and the Lakota, Northern Cheyenne, Arapaho, and others, began in 1850 and continued off and on for forty years.

and the flu to far-flung villages. Because indigenous people had no natural immunity to the germs carried by the traders, the diseases spread rapidly, wiping out whole villages of indigenous people. English colonist Thomas Morton described the results of a smallpox epidemic in a Wampanoag village in 1620: "The hand of God fell heavily upon them, with such a mortal stroke that they died on heaps as they lay in their houses. . . . In a place where many inhabited, there had been but one left to live to tell what became of the rest . . . they were left for crows, kites and vermin to prey upon."[9]

The Death of the Sacred Tree

The traders represented only the beginning of the troubles for North America's indigenous populations. The United States was

Lenapé Clothing and Appearance

When Europeans set foot in America in the 1500s, the Lenapé people were living in the region that now includes New Jersey, Delaware, and Pennsylvania. In his 1994 book, Lenapé chief Hitakonanu'laxk describes the appearance and dress of his people at that time.

> [Our] people were striking to the early Europeans. With long black hair, swarthy to nearly black skin, high prominent cheekbones and painted faces, sometimes with tattoos, our people were comely and handsome. We kept ourselves clean and were very neat in dress and appearance.
>
> Clothing was made from skins, feathers, and plant material, sewn and held together with thread made from sinew. Women wore dresses, men shirts, and both wore leggings, all being made from deerskin. . . . Men and women wore stone and shell pendants, beads, necklaces, armbands and anklets, and earrings of stone, shells, animal teeth and claws. . . .
>
> Hair was worn long by both men and women. It was looked upon as a thing sacred and unique to each person, a kind of signature, placed by the Creator upon each person at birth. It was one's connection to spirit. . . . Tattooing was widely practiced by men and women. A design was drawn and pricked along the outline with a needle until blood was drawn, and then, burnt powdered poplar tree bark was spread thereon.

Hitakonanu'laxk, *The Grandfathers Speak: Native American Folk Tales of the Lenapé People*. New York: Interlink, 1994, pp. 15–16.

created in 1776 out of thirteen colonies on the East Coast, and the nation expanded rapidly in the nineteenth century. By 1848 a group of American states and official territories stretched from the Atlantic coast to the Pacific Ocean. Many of the regions claimed by the federal government were populated by Native Americans who lived as their ancestors had for thousands of years. Indigenous claims to the land meant little to the millions of White farmers, hunters, and gold seekers who swarmed into Native American territories in search of land and riches. White frontier settlements were protected by the US Army, which built hundreds of fortified garrisons across the country.

The final battles on the northern Great Plains, known as the Sioux Wars, began in 1850 and continued off and on for forty years. The wars pitted the US Army against the Lakota, Northern Cheyenne, Arapaho, and others. The Sioux Wars ended in 1890 when five hundred troops of the Seventh Cavalry Regiment massacred one hundred Lakota men, women, and children in a frozen winter battle at Wounded Knee, South Dakota. The slaughter brought a bloody end to nearly three centuries of violent conflict between White Americans and Native Americans.

Oglala Lakota elder Black Elk survived the bloodbath at Wounded Knee. Forty years later Black Elk wrote:

> "The [Lakota] nation's hoop is broken and scattered. There is no center any longer, and the sacred tree is dead."[10]
>
> —Black Elk, Oglala Lakota elder

I did not know then how much was ended. When I look back now from this high hill of my old age, I can still see the butchered women and children lying heaped and scattered all along the crooked gulch. . . . And I can see that something else died there in the bloody mud, and was buried in the blizzard. A people's dream died there. It was a beautiful dream. . . . The nation's hoop is broken and scattered. There is no center any longer, and the sacred tree is dead.[10]

CHAPTER TWO

Rebuilding Communities

In the early 1800s more than 125,000 Native Americans—members of the Cherokee, Chickasaw, Choctaw, Creek, and Seminole nations—lived in Alabama, Georgia, North Carolina, and Tennessee. Like their White neighbors, many of them were farmers. They bought and sold property and other goods. They spoke and read English. Many had even adopted Christianity. Around 1809 a Cherokee silversmith in Georgia named Sequoyah developed a written Cherokee language, the first of its kind. By the 1820s the Cherokee around Dahlonega, Georgia, were publishing the *Cherokee Phoenix* newspaper in both English and Cherokee.

Because they had adopted White ways, the Cherokee, Chickasaw, Choctaw, Creek, and Seminole eventually became known as the Five Civilized Tribes. Despite their willingness to adopt the lifestyle of White Americans, the indigenous peoples of the Southeast were not viewed as equals. Rather, because their communities were built on rich, fertile land, they were seen as obstacles to White prosperity. White farmers were making fortunes growing cotton on huge plantations worked by Black slaves. This attracted thousands of other White settlers eager to build their own farms and businesses. The newcomers wanted the land—and they often got it through violence. They stole cattle, looted homes, and burned towns. In essence, White settlers gained land by destroying thriving Native American communities—and federal and state governments aided these efforts.

The Trail of Tears

President Andrew Jackson supported the actions of the White settlers. Before his election as president in 1828, Jackson had achieved the rank of general in the US Army. He had gained a reputation as a national hero after waging a brutal military campaign that drove the Creek and Seminole from their ancestral lands. In 1830, Jackson signed the Indian Removal Act. That act ordered the relocation of the Five Civilized Tribes from the Southeast to an area that came to be known as Indian Territory in present-day Oklahoma.

In 1831 more than fourteen thousand Choctaw were expelled from their land. Around seven thousand US Army troops rounded up all Choctaw men, women, and children and marched them about 800 miles (1,287 km) west during a frigid winter. Thousands died of starvation, exposure, and diseases like whooping cough, typhus, dysentery, and cholera in what one Choctaw leader called "a trail of tears and death."[11] French historian Alexis de Tocqueville witnessed the brutal removal: "They have lost their country . . . their very families are obliterated; the names they bore in common are forgotten, their language perishes, and all traces of their origin disappear. Their nation has ceased to exist."[12]

The forced removals continued for seven more years. The final act of removal occurred in 1838 when sixteen thousand Cherokee were marched to Oklahoma. An estimated five thousand people died along the way. In a December 1838

By the 1820s the Cherokee around Dahlonega, Georgia, were publishing a newspaper called The Cherokee Phoenix, *which was written in both English and Cherokee.*

speech before Congress, Jackson's successor, President Martin Van Buren, celebrated the forced relocation of the Cherokee people: "It affords sincere pleasure to apprise Congress of the entire removal of the Cherokee Nation of Indians to their new homes west of the Mississippi. The measures authorized by Congress . . . have had the happiest effects."[13]

Rebuilding Starts—and Ends

When the survivors of the Five Civilized Tribes arrived in Indian Country, they were given treaty rights to what is now almost the entire state of Oklahoma, more than 90 million acres (36.4 million ha). The treaty promised the people that they would own the lands forever and trespass by settlers was forbidden. With this agreement in hand, the Cherokee set out to rebuild their community in the northeastern part of the territory. In 1839 the Cherokee Nation adopted a consti-

---

The Cruel Work of Removal

In the late 1880s anthropologist James Mooney interviewed Cherokee who survived the forced march from their homes in the American South to Oklahoma in 1838. An excerpt of Mooney's description of the Trail of Tears, as that march became known, appears here.

> Squads of troops were sent to search out with rifle and bayonet every small cabin hidden away in the coves or by sides of mountain streams, to seize and bring in as prisoners all the occupants, however or wherever they might be found. Families at dinner were startled by the sudden gleam of bayonets in the doorway. . . . Men were seized in their fields or going along the road, women were taken from their [spinning] wheels and children from their play. In many cases, on turning for one last look as they crossed the ridge, they saw their homes in flames, fired by the lawless rabble that followed on the heels of the soldiers to loot and pillage. . . . A Georgia volunteer, afterward a colonel in the Confederate service, said: "I fought through the civil war and have seen men shot to pieces and slaughtered by thousands, but the Cherokee removal was the cruelest work I ever knew."

James Mooney, "Myths of the Cherokee (1902)," Hanover College, 2022. https://history.hanover.edu.

tution and established a government in the town of Tahlequah. They built economic, cultural, and social institutions, including churches, public schools, and colleges. They printed books, pamphlets, and a newspaper called the *Cherokee Advocate*.

The rebuilding of their nation came to an abrupt halt in 1898 after Congress passed the Curtis Act. This law dissolved all Cherokee tribal courts, schools, governments, and land claims in Indian Territory. Communal lands were divided into individual allotments of 160 acres (64.7 ha) per family. Oklahoma became a state in 1907, the same year an oil boom brought thousands of workers to Indian Country. Land swindlers followed, many of them persuading Native American landowners to sign away the rights to their land. According to the Cherokee Nation website, "A dark period of great poverty ensued for many Cherokees, who suddenly had a new government and laws to navigate, as non-Indians quickly acquired former tribal lands. Tribal government trickled but never halted entirely."[14]

Changing Fortunes

The fortunes of the Cherokee Nation—and Native Americans all across the country—took a dramatic turn in 1988 when the federal government passed the Indian Gaming Regulatory Act. The act allowed Native American nations around the country to build large, flashy gambling casinos. The Cherokee opened their first casino in the early 1990s, and millions of dollars began pouring into the community. The money was initially used to open an aerospace equipment manufacturing plant, which continues to employ hundreds of Cherokee workers. Parts made at the factory can be found on the International Space Station.

In 2009 an organization called the Cherokee Nation Businesses (CNB) was founded. This group oversees a growing number of enterprises owned by the community, including hotels, restaurants, casinos, and gas stations. In 2022 the CNB employed more than seventy-five hundred people and had annual revenue of more than $1 billion. The CNB spends around two-thirds of its profits to create jobs, while the rest is invested in health services, education, housing, and other programs in local communities.

One of those programs is the Cherokee Nation Film Office, founded in 2019. The goal of this office is to expand Native American representation in film and TV. In 2022 the film office held a casting call for Native American actors needed for roles on the hit FX series *Reservation Dogs*. Some scenes were also filmed on the reservation. According to Chuck Hoskin Jr., principal chief of the Cherokee Nation, "Cherokee Nation is deeply committed to developing the film and recording industry in Oklahoma. The opportunities for continued growth are substantial. We know it can be a powerful economic tool for creating quality jobs and supporting small, family businesses within the communities of the Cherokee Nation reservation."[15]

> "[The] Cherokee Nation is deeply committed to developing the film and recording industry in Oklahoma.... We know it can be a powerful economic tool for creating quality jobs and supporting small, family businesses."[15]
>
> —Chuck Hoskin Jr., principal chief of the Cherokee Nation

The Long Walk of the Navajo

Few Native American tribes escaped the federal government's systematic destruction of their communities. While some have been able to rebuild, the Navajo, or Diné, Nation has struggled. The Navajo Nation—located in the Four Corners region where Utah, Colorado, Arizona, and New Mexico meet—is the largest reservation in the United States. With over 27,413 square miles (71,000 sq. km), the reservation is larger than West Virginia. Around half of the 399,000 Navajo in the United States live on the reservation.

The Navajo experienced their own version of the Trail of Tears, called the Long Walk. In the early 1860s Navajo clans consisted of ranchers and farmers who occupied large areas of Arizona and western New Mexico. In 1863 the US government tried to persuade around eight thousand Navajo to move from their ancestral lands onto a 40-square-mile (104 sq. km) reservation in eastern

New Mexico called Bosque Redondo. When the clans refused, the US Army engaged in a scorched-earth campaign to eradicate the Navajo way of life. Soldiers slaughtered huge herds of Navajo sheep, destroyed irrigation systems and crops in fields, cut down ancient fruit trees, and burned down villages.

Faced with the prospect of mass starvation in 1864, nearly all Navajo surrendered. They were forced to march 300 miles (483 km) east in eighteen days. The army provided little food or water, and many people lacked the physical strength necessary for the long, hot march. At least two hundred people died on that Long Walk. Conditions at Bosque Redondo were abysmal. The exhausted Navajo were given tainted water to drink, promised food rations that never came, and told to farm in a desert climate that proved nearly impossible. Countless Navajo died under these harsh conditions. However, in 1868 Navajo leaders negotiated a treaty with the US government. That treaty enabled them to establish a reservation in the Four Corners region, the first step toward rebuilding the Navajo Nation. Soon a 10-mile-long (16 km) column of Navajo, followed by large herds of sheep, wound their way back to the land of their ancestors.

In 1831 more than fourteen thousand Choctaw were expelled from their land. Their forced march west during the frigid winter was described by one Choctaw leader as "a trail of tears and death." The final act of removal occurred in 1838 when sixteen thousand Cherokee (pictured) were marched to Oklahoma.

Struggling on the Reservation

Ancestral ties remain strong. Many of the Navajo people who live on the reservation today raise sheep and sell the wool or weave it into blankets and rugs to sell. Some herders and artisans earn a decent living, but many people on the reservation struggle. And casinos are not the answer; the Navajo Nation is too isolated to profit from gaming. According to government figures, 43 percent of families live below the federal poverty line, defined as $27,750 for a family of four in 2022. This is around four times the average poverty rate for the United States. More than one-third of the people live without electricity or telephone landlines. Cell phone signals are so hard to find that the phrase for *cell phone* in the Navajo language loosely translates to "thing you use while running uphill" in search of service.

Forty percent of residents of the reservation lack plumbing and running water. In a 2020 article about reservation life, a Navajo high school freshman referred to as Alice explains, "We have an outhouse out back and we go to the school's gym to take showers when we

The Oneida Rebuild in Wisconsin

The story of the Oneida is a familiar one. The Oneida were originally part of the Haudenosaunee Confederacy in New York. Various treaties signed in the late eighteenth and early nineteenth centuries reduced the Oneida land base from 5 million acres (2 million ha) to only 32 acres (13 ha). Beginning in the 1820s the Oneida began a long walk west, journeying on foot more than 750 miles (1207 km) to northeastern Wisconsin. In Wisconsin the Oneida were able to obtain land from the Winnebago and Menominee, allowing them to preserve their sovereignty. In the early twentieth century, however, a federal law forced the Oneida to divide their land into individual parcels. According to the tribe's public relations director, Bobbi Webster, much of this land was lost to White settlers through "deceit and trickery."

The Oneida were left with a few thousand acres, but the nation was able to open its first gaming operations in Green Bay, Wisconsin, in the late 1980s. Because of its location near a major urban center, the casino was an instant success that transformed the reservation from a place of poverty to a land of prosperity.

Quoted in Hallie Golden, "'Piecing Together a Broken Heart': Native Americans Rebuild Territories They Lost," *The Guardian* (Manchester, UK), February 20, 2021. www.theguardian.com.

More than a third of the members of the Navajo Nation live in poverty without electricity or telephone land lines. While the Navajo people have long been ignored by the federal government, in 2021 the Navajo Nation was allocated billions of dollars by Congress as part of the $1.2 trillion infrastructure bill.

need to."[16] Alice's family hauls water in plastic buckets from wells and livestock tanks about 20 miles (32 km) away from their home. Water must be split between family members and livestock. Alice's family tends fifteen cows, thirty sheep, and four horses.

Education continues to be a challenge for the reservation's young people—and for the tribe as a whole. The high school dropout rate is 44 percent, and only 7 percent of students go on to get a college degree. And getting to school at all can be difficult due to the condition of reservation roads, as journalist Amy Linn explains: "75 percent of the roads are dirt and washboard, most of them studded with rocks and wheel-swallowing potholes. The dirt turns to [mud] in rain and snow; the roads become impassable. School buses can't navigate their routes to pick up children. . . . Many parents don't have cars; they can't deliver kids to school on time, or at all."[17]

Insufficient health care is another major issue, made worse by poor roads and the lack of transportation. The sprawling reservation's ten hospitals are chronically underfunded and overcrowded. Alice describes the hardships: "I remember when my grandmother had to get some medicine a few years ago for her heart and it took forever for the hospital to even see us. There are just so many people waiting to see the doctors in this tiny waiting room."[18]

While the Navajo people have long been ignored by the federal government, that began to change in 2021 when President Joe Biden signed a historic $1.2 trillion infrastructure bill. Navajo

Nation president Jonathan Nez was standing next to Biden on the White House lawn at the official bill signing. The bill will direct $11 billion to the Navajo Nation to pay for broadband internet service, energy upgrades, water, sanitation facilities, road repair, and more. According to Nez, "Infrastructure is the primary building block of our tribal communities. This investment will help rebuild roads and bridges that our people need to access basic services and lay the foundation for many communities to receive broadband and water delivery for the first time."[19]

Buying Back Land

Some tribes are literally rebuilding their communities by buying back the ancestral territories that were taken from them. Since 2000 the Oneida Nation of Wisconsin has been using funds from its gaming operations to buy back two-thirds of its original 65,000-acre (26,305 ha) reservation that had been split into small parcels and sold to people outside the tribe. In addition to funding an expansion of the Oneida's land holdings, gaming profits provide community services. All of the Oneida Nation's 21,300 members receive medical and dental insurance, while students can obtain scholarships for a free college education.

Most Native Americans claim a spiritual connection to the land, and the Oneida plan to keep their new land holdings for all time. As the tribe's public relations director, Bobbi Webster, explained in 2020, "The Oneida Nation needed land to sustain ourselves. . . . Having land is part of our sovereignty."[20] That sovereignty is also necessary for rebuilding communities that have been under attack for more than three centuries. As Alice emphasizes, "Without the rez, I don't think I would be the person I am today. I know that there are some bad things about it but I wouldn't change living there. There is so much community and family here, everyone is connected to everyone else."[21]

> "There is so much community and family [on the Navajo reservation], everyone is connected to everyone else."[21]
>
> —Alice, Navajo high school student

CHAPTER THREE

Reclaiming Identity

In 1769 Spanish soldiers landed in present-day San Diego to claim most of California for Spain. At the time there were about fifty major Native American clans in California, including the Yurok, Chumash, Gabrielino, and Ohlone. The Spanish soldiers were accompanied by Catholic priests of the Franciscan order. The priests had two goals: convert the indigenous people to Christianity and erase their cultural identity. This meant forcing Native Americans to learn European languages, work practices, and culture. In the half century that followed, the Franciscans built a 500-mile (805 km) chain of twenty-one missions from San Diego to Sonoma, north of San Francisco.

The Europeans wished to transform Native Americans into humble, obedient Christians. They were baptized and then enslaved. Spanish was the official language, and priests whipped, starved, and brutally beat men, women, and children who spoke Native languages or engaged in spiritual healing practices. Native oral histories were suppressed and replaced with Bible stories. Christian saints took the place of Native deities.

Diseases killed thousands of so-called Mission Indians, as shown by the grim statistics recorded in official documents. Of the 53,600 Native Americans baptized by mission priests from 1769 to 1845, only 15,000 survived. Within two generations, more than ten thousand years of Native American cultural identity in California was nearly obliterated. Pedro Alcantara, a member of the Ohlone Tribe and a onetime resident of Mission Dolores in San Francisco, despaired. In 1850 he told a historian, "I am very old. My people were once around me like the sands of the shore . . . many . . . many. They have all passed away. . . . I am a Christian Indian. I am all that is left of my people. I am alone."[22]

Boarding Schools

California was granted statehood in 1850, freeing the state's indigenous population from Franciscan control. Life did not improve, however. Native Americans in California and elsewhere were subjected to a new and more insidious assimilation policy—this time carried out by the US government. Beginning in the 1870s tens of thousands of Native American children were forced to attend government-run boarding schools, often called Indian schools. In Riverside, California the Sherman Institute operated much like other such schools. As anthropology professor Lindsay Montgomery explains, "The most traumatic moment for many students was their first entry into these boarding schools, where they were systematically stripped of all outward appearances of 'Indianness.' Their hair was cut. They were given a new outfit. . . . Often their shoes or clothes were too small and they couldn't fit in them properly."[23]

Most Native American boarding schools were based on the model established by the Carlisle Indian Industrial School, which opened in Pennsylvania in 1879. Carlisle was founded by a military officer, Brigadier General Richard Henry Pratt. He believed that the best way to make Native Americans self-sufficient was to force them to abandon their cultural identities. Pratt expressed this belief in his motto: "Kill the Indian and save the man."[24]

Pratt initially recruited children from the Lakota and Dakota Tribes, where extreme hunger and bitter cold ruled daily life. While parents distrusted Pratt, some believed their children would have better lives at the Carlisle boarding school. Some parents had another objective: the United States had a long history of changing treaties to cheat indigenous people out of their land. Native American leaders hoped that teaching their children to read and write English might help them retain their treaty rights.

> "The most traumatic moment for many students was their first entry into these boarding schools, where they were systematically stripped of all outward appearances of 'Indianness.'"[23]
>
> —Lindsay Montgomery, anthropology professor

Beginning in the 1870s, tens of thousands of Native American children were forced to attend schools run by the US government. They were stripped of their traditional life and forced into a non–Native American way of living, including new clothes, language, and short hair.

Carlisle and many other boarding schools were run like military schools. Boys were dressed in military uniforms and made to march in drills like soldiers. Girls wore long Victorian dresses and were trained as nannies, cooks, and housekeepers. Students were given new names—common American names like William and Sarah. They were taught reading, writing, and arithmetic. Instruction was in English only. Sunday church attendance was mandatory. Students were often forbidden to visit parents and families, and letters home went unsent by school officials. Unpaid labor was part of the program. During the two-month summer break, students participated in what was called the outing program; boys worked on local farms while girls worked as domestic servants. Meals were meager, and sexual abuse was common. Many suffered from severe depression, and countless children committed suicide. Diseases like tuberculosis and cholera killed thousands of children, many of whom were buried in unmarked graves.

Officials defended the harsh practices at boarding schools as necessary for assimilating Native Americans. But as historian Roxanne Dunbar-Ortiz writes, the schools were a failure: "Although stripped of the languages and skills of their communities, what they learned in boarding school was useless for the purposes of effective assimilation, creating multiple lost generations of traumatized individuals."[25]

Carlisle closed in 1918, but the Bureau of Indian Affairs (BIA) continued to run boarding schools for decades. Attendance peaked in 1973, when over sixty thousand Native American children attended one of the 226 BIA schools operating in seventeen states. In 1978 Congress passed the Indian Child Welfare Act, which allowed parents to

> "What [indigenous children] learned in boarding school was useless for the purposes of effective assimilation, creating multiple lost generations of traumatized individuals."[25]
>
> —Roxanne Dunbar-Ortiz, historian

Investigating Boarding Schools

In 2022 the Department of Interior released a report after investigating more than four hundred boarding schools that were in operation in the United States from 1820s to the 1970s. The investigative report confirmed that Native American children in these schools often faced hunger, disease, and cruel punishments. Thousands of children died from abuse, sickness, accidents, and suicide. The dead were interred in graves that were often left unmarked; burial sites have been found at more than fifty different boarding school locations across the country. In some cases, parents were never told that their children had died.

When Secretary of the Interior Deb Haaland launched the initiative in 2021 she explained why this painful chapter in American history must be brought to the public's attention:

> The consequences of federal Indian boarding school policies—including the intergenerational trauma caused by the family separation and cultural eradication inflicted upon generations of children as young as 4 years old—are heartbreaking and undeniable. . . . It is my priority to not only give voice to the survivors and descendants of federal Indian boarding school policies, but also to address the lasting legacies of these policies so Indigenous peoples can continue to grow and heal.

Deb Haaland, "Department of the Interior Releases Investigative Report, Outlines Next Steps in Federal Indian Boarding School Initiative," US Department of the Interior, May 11, 2022. www.doi.gov.

keep their kids out of BIA schools. Since that time Native Americans have worked to reverse the cultural legacies they lost in the boarding school system.

The Importance of Language

One of those lost cultural legacies is language. The spoken and written language of all Native American boarding schools was English. The use of indigenous languages was prohibited. Children who lapsed into their Native languages were punished. As a result, over time countless young Native Americans lost the ability to speak and understand the languages of their parents and grandparents. The damage to indigenous cultures was profound. Many Native Americans believe that ceremonies, prayers, and stories can only be communicated in Native languages. Therefore, those who do not know their language cannot understand their cultural heritage or identity. Anton Treuer is trying to reverse such losses. Treuer, who was born in 1969 to a White father and an Ojibwa mother, grew up on the Leech Lake Reservation outside Bemidji in northern Minnesota. He faced extreme racial discrimination while attending high school in Bemidji, where he says he was "spoon-fed out of a bucket of whiteness every day."[26]

Treuer went on to attend Princeton University and the University of Minnesota, where he earned a doctorate in history. After college Treuer returned to the reservation, where he focused on becoming fluent in the Ojibwa language. He worked with Ojibwa elder Archie Mosay to learn complex prayers, songs, rituals, and ceremonies. Treuer believes these rituals can only be performed properly in the Ojibwa language. He says, "Changing [a] ceremony and doing it in English would lose a lot of the nuanced meaning and some of the spiritual force. I really believe that the language is a powerful tool to keep us recognizable to our ancestors. . . . To circumvent that process would lose the spiritual dimension."[27]

Treuer became a professor of the Ojibwa language at Bemidji State University in 2000. He also travels to Wisconsin to teach at the Waadookodaading Ojibwe Language Immersion School on the

Some Native Americans are working to help youngsters become fluent speakers of their language. These children study at Waadookodaading Ojibwe Language Immersion School.

Lac Courte Oreilles Indian Reservation. In addition to being one of a small group of indigenous language professors, Treuer has written or edited more than a dozen books about Native American languages and culture. He also founded the *Oshkaabewis Native Journal* in 2000, the only academic journal written in the Ojibwa language. Through his work as a "language warrior," Treuer has helped hundreds of students become fluent speakers of Ojibwa. To further his goal of helping young Native Americans understand their heritage and reclaim their identity, he often makes this request of his students: "If you learn something—a song, a medicine, a word—make sure you teach it to at least four other people."[28]

> "If you learn something—a song, a medicine, a word—make sure you teach it to at least four other people."[28]
>
> —Anton Treuer, professor of Ojibwa language and culture

Powwow Dreams

Beyond the classroom, many Native American traditions are shared at powwows (also written as pow wows and pow-wows). Native Americans believe in the healing power of song, dance, and drumming. All of these are featured at powwows, which provide an opportunity for people to come together to honor their culture and identity.

The roots of the modern powwow can be traced to a time before colonization, when each Native American clan had its own unique ceremonies, songs, dances, decorative clothing, and body decorations. Some of these practices can be traced to the special religious organizations, or societies, that were part of almost every clan. Members of the Iroquois False Face Society, for instance, wore extravagantly carved masks while conducting healing ceremonies. In the southern plains, the Grass Dance Society was made up of warriors from Omaha, Pawnee, and other clans who affirmed their connection to the spirits by swaying like prairie grasses during ceremonial dances.

Keeping Art Traditions Alive

Native Americans have been using natural elements to create beautiful and practical artworks for thousands of years. In the twenty-first century, some are keeping ancient traditions alive through their art. Choctaw/Cherokee artist Jeffrey Gibson employs traditional handcraft techniques like basket weaving, glass beading, and colorful porcupine quillwork to create remarkable collages and sculptures.

In northern New York, Mohawk weaver Carrie Hill makes traditional Haudenosaunee baskets from black ash and sweetgrass using techniques learned from her aunt. Using these skills, Hill creates woven face masks, jewelry, and other items. Hill also teaches workshops, as explained on her website: "Carrie is a teacher of Haudenosaunee Fancy Basketry to pre-kindergarten aged children all the way to Totas (Grandparents). Carrie finds honor and pleasure in doing so both in educational environments and community gatherings. She is very proud to pass along this ancient tradition to her children, her community and the next generations of artistic leaders."

Carrie Hill, "Workshops," Chill Baskets, 2022. http://chill-baskets.com.

Spiritual societies place great importance on visions and prophetic dreams. The word *powwow* itself comes from the Algonquian word *pau wau*, which translates to "he dreams." In the early twentieth century, an Ojibwa elder experienced a series of dreams that inspired a modern powwow tradition. The elder dreamed of four women wearing dresses decorated with four rows of metal jingles that rang sweetly when they danced. After the man described the dreams to his wife, she created what is known as a jingle dress using rolled-up tin lids from tobacco cans. She passed along the idea to other women, who made their own dresses that jingled when they danced.

At the time, ritualistic dancing and other traditional spiritual ceremonies on reservations were prohibited by US laws. When

Many Native American traditions are shared at powwows, community gatherings where people honor their culture and identity.

women began performing the jingle dress dance, it was seen as a radical act. In 1978 President Jimmy Carter signed the American Indian Religious Freedom Act, which lifted restrictions against Native American cultural and spiritual practices. Within a few years powwows became extremely popular. Today the jingle dress dance is one of the most beloved of the women's dances at Ojibwa powwows and elsewhere. Modern young people have added their own spin to powwow dance traditions with, for instance, hip-hop hoop dancing. This athletic performance features dancers who rapidly spin, juggle, and link as many as ten hoops as rap music plays.

The biggest powwow is the annual Gathering of Nations, held every April at the Powwow Grounds in Albuquerque, New Mexico. Dancers in beads, feathers, and elaborate costumes made of velvet, buckskin, fringe, and feathers come together to compete in thirty-five dance categories that include age groups from Tiny Tots to Elders over seventy. The powwow features singing, drumming, horse and rider parades, cultural displays, and seminars in which elders teach ancient wisdom in their Native language. The Indian Traders Market hosts indigenous merchants of arts, crafts, and souvenirs.

The traditions honored at powwow that were once considered illegal by the US government have helped Native Americans reclaim their identities. As Treuer sees it, "Five hundred years ago, Europeans came to America and announced, 'Those Indians ain't gonna last.' They've kept saying it every year since. And for five hundred years in a row, the Europeans have been wrong. There is nothing as powerful as a living tribal language to prove that point."[29]

CHAPTER FOUR

Striving for Rights

Native Americans governed themselves as self-ruling, or sovereign, nations for millennia. When indigenous people were forced to surrender their lands to the United States, they negotiated treaties as members of sovereign nations. Treaties are legal documents. They guaranteed that each tribal nation would exist as an independent entity within the borders of the United States. Native American nations created their own governments, laws, schools, and social services. Treaty rights allowed tribes to manage their own lands and natural resources.

The legal definition of sovereign Native American nations was enshrined in more than five hundred treaties. But in 1953 Congress passed a sweeping law called the Indian Termination Act that ended, or terminated, the sovereign status of 109 tribes. As Cheyenne leader and Colorado senator Ben Nighthorse Campbell stated in 2007, "In Washington's infinite wisdom, it was decided that tribes should no longer be tribes, never mind that they had been tribes for thousands of years."[30]

The termination act ended federal assistance that paid for health, education, and employment programs while extinguishing fishing and hunting rights for the targeted tribes. The idea behind termination was to force Native Americans to move off reservations so they could be assimilated into White culture. Author Max Nesterak explains why politicians were eager to pass the act: "The vision was that eventually there would be no more [BIA], no more tribal governments, no more reservations, and no more Native Americans."[31]

When the act was passed, some Native American nations immediately lost their sovereign status. These nations included the Flathead in Montana, the Klamath in the Pacific Northwest, and the Menominee, Potawatomi, and Chippewa (Ojibwa) in the Midwest. Other tribes targeted for termination resided in California, Texas, New York, and Florida.

Losing Rights to Termination

The Indian Termination Act allowed the BIA to end all health care services to terminated tribes, resulting in sixty reservation hospitals being closed. Schools that had been run by tribal governments were closed. Educational matters were turned over to state governments, which often did not have the money or desire to educate indigenous students. On the Menominee Indian Reservation in Wisconsin, termination resulted in school closings that left about 75 percent of students with no way to continue their education.

Despite the lack of services, termination allowed states to levy income taxes, property taxes, and other fees on Native Americans for the first time. Many could not afford to pay taxes. They lost their homes and were pushed further into poverty. Termination also meant that the government could sell off large parcels of tribal

US senator Ben Nighthorse Campbell of Colorado criticized the Indian Termination Act, which eliminated the sovereign status of over one hundred Native American tribes.

land that held a wealth of natural resources like timber, oil, and minerals. The businesses that benefited from those resources, such as sawmills and mines, closed. These closures left many reservation residents without jobs. Native American law specialist Stephen L. Pevar saw the damage caused by the Indian Termination Act: "Nothing causes tribes and their members to lose more rights than termination. [Termination] is the ultimate weapon of Congress and ultimate fear of tribes."[32] As a result of this Act, about twelve thousand Native Americans lost their official tribal status. They also lost 1.3 million acres (526,091 ha) of reservation lands.

> "Nothing causes tribes and their members to lose more rights than termination. [Termination] is the ultimate weapon of Congress and ultimate fear of tribes."[32]
>
> —Stephen L. Pevar, Native American law specialist

Relocating to Big Cities

The government goal of assimilating Native Americans into mainstream US culture continued in 1956 with the passage of the Indian Relocation Act. The law authorized the BIA to pay Native American families a few hundred dollars if they volunteered to move to big cities like Los Angeles, San Francisco, Cleveland, Chicago, Denver, and Minneapolis. At the time only 8 percent of Native Americans lived in cities. Government flyers that promoted relocation promised good jobs, schools, and housing to those who took part in the program. The reality was quite different for the one hundred thousand Native Americans who volunteered to move to cities from 1956 to 1970.

When the Indian Relocation Act was passed, reservation life was little different than it had been in the nineteenth century. Most Native Americans on reservations were poor, but they were surrounded by their own people. Many of those who moved to the cities felt isolated and alone. They were called racist slurs and denied good jobs and decent housing. In the mid-1960s ten-year-old Clovia Malatre moved from the Pine Ridge Reservation in South Dakota to Chicago, where she still lives. "I hated it here," she says.

Struggles with Life in the City

Charlotte and Clyde Day, along with their six children, exemplify the problems faced by those who participated in the Indian Relocation Act. The Days lived on the rural Ojibwa reservation in northern Minnesota, where Clyde was renowned for his skills as a hunter, trapper, fisher, and canoe builder. Charlotte, like many others on the reservation, chopped firewood, hauled water, and washed the family clothes in a river.

In 1964 the Day family boarded a train to Cleveland with a few hundred dollars provided by the BIA. The Days could only afford to move into a two-bedroom apartment in Cleveland's poorest neighborhood, which was marked by crime, racial violence, and pollution. Clyde could only find a job washing dishes; it did not pay enough to support his family. The Days wanted to return home after one month, but they could not afford return tickets. The family eventually made its way back to the reservation, but Clyde began drinking as he struggled to start over. Eventually, the Day family broke up. Charlotte moved to St. Paul with three of the children, while two of the siblings moved to Seattle as part of the BIA relocation program. Thousands of other Native American families experienced similar shock and trauma after they splintered during the relocation program.

"It was so different from being on the reservation where you are primarily living with Indian people, speaking Indian. . . . I remember being in the classroom and deathly afraid of the teacher calling on me because I could not pronounce any of the words."[33]

Aiming for Dignity

The relocation program had one positive effect. In the mid-1960s urban Native Americans began organizing and protesting in order to gain equal rights. These efforts were inspired in part by the Black Power movement. Black Power was popularized in 1966 by Black activist Stokely Carmichael, who defined it as "a call for black people in this country to unite, to recognize their heritage, to build a sense of community. It is a call for black people to define their own goals, to lead their own organizations."[34]

> "I remember being in the classroom and deathly afraid of the teacher calling on me because I could not pronounce any of the words."[33]
>
> —Clovia Malatre, relocated Native American woman

The idea of coming together to promote their culture and build stronger ties among Native American nations appealed to a group of Ojibwa activists in the Twin Cities of Minneapolis–St. Paul. In 1968 Clyde Bellecourt, Dennis Banks, George Mitchell, and Eddie Benton Banai founded the American Indian Movement (AIM) to combat police harassment and violence. AIM members Paul Chaat Smith and Robert Allen Warrior describe the group's original activities: "AIM raised money to equip cars with two-way radios, cameras and tape recorders so they could monitor arrests by the police department. When the AIM Patrol heard police dispatched to certain bars or street corners, officers would be met by Indians in red jackets carefully observing their actions."[35]

The Twin Cities attracted many who participated in the relocation program. The reservations in northern Minnesota were close enough to the Twin Cities that Native people could travel back and forth. As the Twin Cities Native American population swelled, AIM began to grow rapidly. Ojibwa Dorene Day says her mother, Charlotte, was eager to join AIM to protest "the rat-infested dilapidated housing that Indian people were living in. Any time there was a situation where the community was being called together to stand up for our rights, she was there."[36]

Occupying Alcatraz Island

With the relocation program in full force, AIM chapters were founded in cities across the country. During a period when the United States was wracked by urban uprisings, assassinations, and anti–Vietnam War demonstrations, Native American protests might have gone unnoticed. But in November 1969 the group made international headlines when around eighty Native American activists took over Alcatraz Island in San Francisco Bay. The 12-acre (4.9 ha) island was the site of the infamous Alcatraz Federal Penitentiary until its numerous buildings were abandoned 1963.

The Alcatraz takeover was sparked by two California college students, Anthony Garcia, an Apache, and Dennis Turner, a member of the Rincon band. The men felt that the state's education

In 1969 activists from the American Indian Movement (AIM) occupied Alcatraz Island in San Francisco Bay to publicize the California education system's neglect of Native American students' needs.

system neglected the needs of Native American students. They wanted universities to hire more indigenous teachers and offer more courses highlighting Native American contributions to mainstream knowledge and culture. The activists viewed the Alcatraz takeover as a way to draw attention to these issues.

For the purpose of the protest, Garcia and Turner formed a group called Indians of All Tribes (IOAT). The IOAT provided a legal justification for the takeover by citing the 1868 Treaty of Fort Laramie (Wyoming) that the US government made with the Great Sioux Nation. The treaty stated that any forts, prisons, or federal lands that were out of use or abandoned would be returned to Indians.

The Alcatraz takeover brought the attention Garcia and Turner had hoped to attract. Hordes of reporters descended on Alcatraz Island to write about the occupation. Smith and Warrior describe the situation: "The press shared the sentiment that the occupation was history in the making and Alcatraz rode an ocean of good will that seemed boundless. The whirlwind of media attention left Indians of All Tribes with a growing tide of donated money, food, and clothing."[37] By January 1970 the occupiers were printing a daily newsletter. Santee Dakota activist John Trudell broadcast a thirty-minute

New Laws and New Rights

The Native American occupation of Alcatraz Island attracted attention at the highest levels of government. In the years that followed, Congress passed sixteen major pieces of legislation that granted new rights to Native Americans. The new laws include the Indian Education Act of 1972, which increased funding for eleven hundred Native American school districts. The Indian Self-Determination and Education Assistance Act of 1975 returned self-governance to Indian nations. This act granted many rights, including allowing tribes to determine where children went to school and how natural resources on their land would be used. One of the most important laws was the American Indian Religious Freedom Act of 1978, which gave Native Americans the right to practice religious and cultural traditions that had been outlawed for more than a century. A change in BIA policy allowed nations to reverse termination by applying for federal recognition. In the twenty years that followed, over 350 tribes took advantage of this right.

program, *Radio Free Alcatraz*, five days a week on public radio stations in San Francisco, Los Angeles, and New York City.

As the takeover stretched on for months, the government sought ways to evict the occupiers. In May 1970 officials shut off electrical power to the island. This cut the freshwater supply that was provided to the island from electric pumps. As the months passed it became increasingly difficult to live on Alcatraz Island, and many occupiers left. The takeover continued into 1971, but the media and the public had long since moved on to other stories. In June a large contingent of federal police officers stormed the island and evicted the last fifteen people who occupied Alcatraz Island.

Regaining Rights

The nineteen-month occupation of Alcatraz Island marked the beginning of many changes in government policy, as Smith and Warrior write: "[Indian activists] saw more attention lavished on their community in the first few weeks of the occupation than had ever occurred in their lifetimes, and knew that attention could be parleyed into something—a new community center, job training . . . and more."[38] Some of the changes were made before the occupation ended. In July 1970 President Richard Nixon called on the BIA to halt enforcement of the Indian Termination Act.

Congress also proceeded to pass sixteen laws to improve Native American education, health, housing, and tribal governance. In 2018 Lumbee Tribe writer and educator Dean Chavers wrote, "[These] federal laws and programs have started to improve life for Indians on reservations. But . . . it will take several generations to make life significantly better for Indian people. So while many people thought we were crazy for taking over an island prison in San Francisco Bay, the changes that protest set in motion have been positive and long-lasting."[39]

After Alcatraz, AIM addressed the rights and needs of Native American communities in other ways. The movement founded the Little Earth housing project in Minneapolis in 1973. The 9.4 acre (3.8 ha), 212-unit housing complex provides low-cost housing and other services to around sixteen hundred indigenous people. In 1978 AIM organized an event called the Longest Walk, a 3,200-mile (5,150 km) walk from San Francisco to Washington, DC, to protest eleven federal bills that threatened treaty rights. The AIM walk was a success, and the bills were defeated.

> "While many people thought we were crazy for taking over [the Alcatraz Island] prison in San Francisco Bay, the changes that protest set in motion have been positive and long-lasting."[39]
>
> —Dean Chavers, Native American writer and educator

Fighting for Environmental Justice

In the twenty-first century, environmental justice in general, and climate change in particular, are a central focus for many Native American activists. Tom Goldtooth, founder of the Indigenous Environmental Network, is one of these activists. He says, "Populations such as ours that have a close relationship with nature . . . are experiencing these real effects, from Alaska to many of our tribal people here in the lower 48 [states]."[40]

Tom and his son Dallas addressed some of the major environmental issues affecting Native Americans when they organized the Dakota Access Pipeline (DAPL) protests that made headlines in 2016. The grassroots protest movement tried to prevent construction of a $3.7 billion crude oil pipeline in western North Dakota. In addition to transporting climate-warming fossil fuel, the pipeline directly threatened the freshwater supply of the Standing Rock Indian Reservation, home to the Standing Rock Sioux Tribe. The DAPL was designed to pass under the Missouri River less than 1 mile (1.6 km) from the reservation.

In April 2016 LaDonna Brave Bull Allard of the Standing Rock Sioux Tribe and her grandchildren had set up camp near the pipeline construction site in preparation for their protest. By the end

In 2016 Native Americans from an estimated three hundred tribes set up camp to protest construction of the Dakota Access Pipeline, which they considered a threat to water supplies on the Standing Rock Indian Reservation.

of the month, Native Americans from an estimated three hundred tribes throughout the country had come to the camp to protest for environmental justice. This was the largest gathering of Native American nations in a century. By summer the demonstration had attracted an estimated thirty-five hundred protesters of all races and backgrounds.

As the protests intensified, thirty young Standing Rock Sioux formed a group called ReZpect Our Water. They collected 140,000 signatures on a petition to stop the pipeline and organized a relay race to deliver the petition to President Barack Obama in Washington, DC. In August 2016 the three-week, 2,000-mile (3,219 km) run from North Dakota culminated with dozens of young Native Americans singing, drumming, and marching in front of the White House. While the protests failed to stop the pipeline, Jasilyn Charger of the Cheyenne River Sioux Tribe eloquently summed up the decades-long fight Native Americans have waged for justice and to regain their rights: "It's up to us to hold our government accountable. Our land is in danger, as well as our identity, but we will not stand in silence. We are . . . uniting [Indian] nations that have been separate for generations. We must take advantage of this chance to make a change."[41]

While some who face environmental catastrophes can move elsewhere, Native Americans have a spiritual connection to their ancestral lands that goes back thousands of years. This relationship with the land links environmental justice to maintaining tribal sovereignty, protecting sacred sites and practices, and regaining basic human rights that have been brutally curtailed for centuries.

CHAPTER FIVE

Confronting Challenges

Maria Yellow Horse Brave Heart is an Oglala Lakota and a mental health expert. For two decades beginning in the 1980s, Brave Heart conducted psychological research among the Lakota people in North and South Dakota. This brought her to a new understanding of difficulties that have long plagued Native American communities. She concluded that Native Americans experience historical trauma. She defines this as an "emotional and psychological wounding"[42] passed down from one generation to the next.

The mental anguish and unresolved grief of historical trauma has been intensifying since the seventeenth century. According to Brave Heart, the first contact by Europeans shattered traditional Native societies with the introduction of alcohol and disease. In the nineteenth century psychological wounds were experienced by those who survived mass extermination and dislocation from their homes. The reservation period that followed caused deep soul wounds among Native Americans who depended on their oppressors—the US government—for basic survival.

The boarding school period—marked by beatings, sexual abuse, and the prohibition of Native languages and culture—resulted in more historical trauma. Traditional indigenous family support systems were further destroyed by forced relocation and tribal termination, which traumatized those who lost community and economic security. As Brave Heart wrote in 1998, this cumulative historical trauma "contributes to the current social pathology of high rates of suicide, homicide, domestic violence, child abuse, alcoholism and other social problems among American Indians."[43]

Ongoing Trauma

The problems Brave Heart described in the late twentieth century continue to haunt Native American communities. This was affirmed in 2022 by Joseph Ojibway, a psychiatric nurse at the Saginaw Chippewa Indian Tribe medical clinic in Michigan. Ojibway describes the psychological problems he sees among older clients who attended boarding school as children:

> They're coming in now as adults and often times they're still struggling, whether it be with addiction, chronic depression, anxiety. It's a result of historical trauma that's been built up and passed on and is just coming to the surface. They might not be fully aware that it's related to the long lineage of suffering and experiences that their ancestors have gone through. But that's how I recognize it.[44]

Historical trauma continues to take a toll on Native American lives. The rate of substance abuse is higher among Native Americans than among any other population group in the country, according to the National Survey on Drug Use and Health. Around 12 percent of the Native American population engages in heavy alcohol use (more than four drinks per day), compared to 8 percent for Whites and 6 percent for Latinos. Methamphetamine use is three times the rate of any other group. Native Americans are also more likely to commit suicide, according to the Centers for Disease Control and Prevention. While the US suicide rate increased 33 percent from 1999 to 2020, the rate of suicide among Native American men grew by 71 percent during that period. For indigenous women,

> "[Historical trauma] contributes to the ... high rates of suicide, homicide, domestic violence, child abuse, alcoholism and other social problems among American Indians."[43]
>
> —Maria Yellow Horse Brave Heart, mental health expert

According to mental health expert Maria Yellow Horse Brave Heart, Native Americans experience historical trauma, which she defines as "emotional and psychological wounding" passed down from one generation to the next.

the suicide rate during those years rose by 139 percent. Experts blame the high rate of suicide among women on domestic violence. According to the US Department of Justice, 84 percent of American Indian girls and women experience domestic violence in their lifetimes; around 33 percent are victims of sexual violence, about double the number for White women. According to the US Department of Justice, the problem is worse in Alaska, where the rate of domestic violence and sexual assault among Native women is ten times that of women in the rest of the country.

Many Native women experience violence at the hands of non-Native perpetrators (over 50 percent of Native women are married to non-Native men). These non-Native men, including husbands, boyfriends, and government and religious authorities, often live on tribal lands. And most non-Native offenders evade prosecution because of the complex web of laws that govern reservations. In many places tribal police and courts have no authority over non-Indians. State and federal authorities like the Federal Bureau of Investigation and the BIA must be called in to prosecute non-Indians for reservation crimes. This rarely happens, and non-Indian men often evade prosecution for domestic violence, rape, and other crimes committed on reservations.

Young people who witness violence often develop post-traumatic stress disorder (PTSD). According to a report commissioned by the US Department of Justice, Native American children experience PTSD at the same rate as combat veterans who fought in wars in Iraq and Afghanistan. This is triple the rate of the general population. The report says PTSD results in nightmares, depression, poor physical health, poor school performance, and substance abuse. It is also why suicide is a leading cause of death for young Native Americans. More than one-third of all Native American suicides are among young people aged ten to twenty-four.

Ongoing Trauma

Sociologist Les B. Whitbeck conducted one of the few academic studies to measure the effects of historical trauma on Native Americans. Whitbeck held focus groups with several hundred Native Americans in the upper Midwest. His 2004 study determined that 36 percent of Native Americans thought about the loss of traditional languages and the loss of their culture every day. Twenty-four percent reported feeling angry regarding historical losses, and nearly half said they had disturbing thoughts related to these losses. Around one-quarter of those interviewed said they felt uncomfortable around White people, while a third were distrustful of White culture. Whitbeck explained the findings:

> The holocaust is not over for many American Indian people. It continues to affect their perceptions on a daily basis and impinges on their psychological and physical health. . . . The threats to their way of life and culture have been ongoing, the losses progressive as each generation passes away. These losses are so salient because they are not truly "historical" in the sense that they are now in the past. Rather they are "historical" in the sense that they began a long time ago. . . . The losses are not over. They are continuing day by day.

Les B. Whitbeck et al., "Conceptualizing and Measuring Historical Trauma Among American Indian People," *American Journal of Community Psychology*, June 2004. www.mcgill.ca.

Handing Down Wisdom

The numbers paint a bleak picture of the ongoing challenges faced by Native Americans. But lives have been saved by the pioneering work of Brave Heart and others who have developed solutions to multigenerational trauma. These solutions are based on traditional indigenous cultural values. The Culture Forward program, developed by the Center for American Indian Health (CAIH), connects tribal elders with young people. The goal is to prevent youth suicide by strengthening connections to tribal identity and cultural values.

In northwestern Alaska CAIH Culture Camps focus on young people who are experiencing a number of challenges, including historical trauma, poverty, and substance abuse. Kids camp at remote sites, where elders teach indigenous languages and guide groups through healing rituals and other activities. Another Culture Forward program that connects young people with elders focuses on rug weaving. This work is both practical and symbolic. While rugs can be sold, they are also seen as a tapestry that represents the dreams of the weaver. As Secretary of the Interior Deb Haaland explained in 2019, "The stories that are told to us as children are woven into our baskets, rugs, and blankets and exchanged across space and time. These weavings explain where we came from and who we are. . . . Although our weavings tell stories that are not written, they are authored by us and illustrate a story that tells us that our people are survivors and that we are resilient."[45]

> "Although our weavings tell stories that are not written, they are authored by us and illustrate a story that tells us that our people are survivors and that we are resilient."[45]
>
> —Deb Haaland, secretary of the interior

Climate Change Challenges

Native Americans often look to the land as a source of healing. Many believe the natural world is home to ancestors and spirits

Salmon have played a central role in the life of members of the Tulalip Nation, who live near the shores of Puget Sound. Salmon provide a steady source of food, but the river waters where salmon spawn have heated up as the climate warms. This has caused salmon populations to plunge in recent decades.

whose power can restore and sustain mental and physical health. Native American women call this ideal state of well-being walking in beauty. According to alternative health professionals Mary Koithan and Cynthia Farrell, "Walking in beauty . . . requires a close connection to the earth and living in harmony with the environment."[46]

Koithan and Farrell explain that spiritual ceremonies and physical practices, such as running each morning to greet the dawn, have been used for thousands of years in traditional Native American medicine. But as threats from climate change continue to grow, it has become more difficult to live in harmony with the earth. In Arizona water wells that the Navajo have relied on for centuries are drying up due to the worst western drought in the past twelve hundred years. In Alaska the warming climate is melting the ice in the soil called permafrost, turning long-frozen land into soggy mud. This has forced the Yupik people to abandon their ancestral villages as softened ground causes buildings to collapse.

These new challenges are driving Native American efforts to restore and heal the environment on reservations across the

Moving to Stop the Violence

Native Americans, especially women, go missing and are murdered at a higher rate than other Americans. The problem is so common that it spurred the formation of the missing and murdered indigenous peoples (MMIP) movement. Grassroots MMIP activists, who are often victims and their families, are pushing governments to dedicate more resources to the issue. The majority of MMIP cases are under the jurisdiction of the Federal Bureau of Investigation and the BIA. But a 2021 government study revealed that federal agents are often uninterested in investigations due to historic and systemic racism against Native Americans, especially women.

In the Navajo Nation Eugenia Charles-Newton is working to raise awareness. In 2002, when she was a teenager, Charles-Newton was beaten and sexually assaulted for days by a man who was never arrested or prosecuted. Charles-Newton hopes the new focus on violence against Native American women can prevent others from going through a similar ordeal. She says, "I know that it's going to be a long time before something like that happens. But at the same time, I think that there are some who have convinced me that as long as we keep working together, and as long as we keep talking about these things, change will happen."

Quoted in Henry Gass, "Missing Indigenous Women: Activists Spur a Reckoning," *Christian Science Monitor*, June 6, 2022. www.csmonitor.com.

country. Nikki Cooley is the Navajo co-manager of the Tribes & Climate Change Program in Flagstaff, Arizona. She says, "Tribes have always been adapting to climate change. Now we have to adapt even faster. . . . We put our non-human relatives first, meaning the trees, the sky, the water. We don't treat them as objects to be studied in a lab. We revere them."[47]

On the shores of Puget Sound in Washington, the Swinomish are fighting back against the threat posed by ocean acidification. This problem is caused by excess carbon dioxide in the atmosphere, which is produced by the burning of fossil fuels. The oceans are absorbing carbon dioxide and becoming more acidic, a condition that threatens clams, crabs, and other shellfish.

Seafood is a staple for many of the one thousand people living on the Swinomish Reservation. To boost clam numbers, the Swinomish are reviving an ancient practice called clam gardening. Clam gardeners build low rock walls, around 2 feet high (61 cm), along beaches at low tide. Sand piles up behind the walls, creating a gentle slope that makes for ideal clam habitat. Shaping hundreds of heavy rocks into a wall is hard work. But building clam gardens provides a reliable food source, along with a sense of purpose for young people who participate in the project. As Swinomish official Joseph Williams says, "There've been times I've been really negative looking forward. . . . [But] as long as we keep our kids excited about taking care of our environment, things remain optimistic."[48]

> "As long as we keep our kids excited about taking care of our environment, things remain optimistic."[48]
>
> —Joseph Williams, Swinomish official

The four thousand members of the Tulalip Tribes live in the same coastal region as the Swinomish. Salmon have played a central role in Tulalip life and culture for millennia. Salmon provide a steady source of food, while salmon spirits are said to connect the Tulalip people to their ancestors. But the river waters where salmon spawn have heated up as the climate warms. This has caused salmon populations to plunge in recent decades.

The Tulalip have hit on a natural solution to restore the ecological and spiritual balance provided by salmon. They are reintroducing beavers to reservation rivers. In the nineteenth century, beavers were trapped to near extinction. But the beaver dams built from trees and brush provide great benefits to river ecosystems.

Members of the Tulalip Nation have reintroduced beavers to the reservation's rivers. The dams the beavers build create ponds that cool the river waters, which improves conditions for salmon spawning.

The ponds that form behind the dams help cool river waters, making ideal spawning habitat for salmon and other aquatic creatures.

Healing the Earth and the People

Healing the environment can help heal the community, as psychiatrist Marcello Maviglia writes:

> Native Americans' concerted effort to preserve the environment is a form of "communal therapy" and a way to overcome the negative sequels of Historical Trauma. . . . The work by Indigenous scholars. . . . stresses the role of traditional values, including the respect and realignment with the land and "mother earth" as a healing path for the psychological damage inflicted on Native population.[49]

Many in the modern world have forgotten what Native Americans have long understood: that the link between mother earth and humanity cannot be ruptured without dire consequences. Research has shown that widespread environmental destruction increases physical and mental problems in all people. By confronting environmental problems in a clear-sighted manner, Native Americans are working to reverse centuries of historical trauma while preparing for an uncertain future.

> "Native Americans' . . . effort to preserve the environment is a form of 'communal therapy' and a way to overcome the negative sequels of Historical Trauma."[49]
>
> —Marcello Maviglia, psychiatrist

SOURCE NOTES

Introduction: Unique Cultures, Diverse People

1. Kevin Gover, "Five Myths About American Indians," *Washington Post*, November 22, 2017. www.washingtonpost.com.
2. Robert Martin, "To Lead Is to Serve," Tribal College, February 20, 2022. https://tribalcollegejournal.org.
3. Quoted in Roxanne Dunbar-Ortiz, "Yes, Native Americans Were the Victims of Genocide," History News Network, May 12, 2016. https://historynewsnetwork.org.

Chapter One: Early Life in America

4. Quoted in Charles C. Mann, *1491*. New York: Vintage, 2006, p. 14.
5. Quoted in "Native Teachings Are About a Way of Life," Anishnawbe Mushkiki, 2022. https://mushkiki.com/our-programs/clans.
6. Quoted in Charles C. Mann, "1491," *The Atlantic*, March 2002. www.theatlantic.com.
7. Roxanne Dunbar-Ortiz, *The Indigenous Peoples' History of the United States.* Boston: Beacon, 2015, p. 25.
8. Lewis Henry Morgan, *The League of the Ho-dé-no-sau-nee or Iroquois.* New York: Citadel, 1993, p. 155.
9. Thomas Morton, "Thomas Morton: Manners and Customs of the Indians (of New England), 1637," Fordham University, January 20, 2021. https://sourcebooks.fordham.edu.
10. Black Elk et al., *Black Elk Speaks.* New York: SUNY Press, 2008, p. 218.

Chapter Two: Rebuilding Communities

11. Quoted in Len Greenwood, "Trail of Tears from Mississippi Walked by Our Ancestors," School of Choctaw Language, 2017. https://choctawschool.com.
12. Alexis de Tocqueville, "Democracy in America," Pearson, 2022. https://wps.pearsoncustom.com.
13. Martin Van Buren, "State of the Union Address: Martin Van Buren (December 3, 1838)," Infoplease, 2022. www.infoplease.com.
14. Cherokee Nation, "History," 2022. www.cherokee.org.
15. Chuck Hoskin Jr., "Check Out Our Sound Stage," Cherokee Nation Film Office, 2021. https://cherokee.film.

16. Quoted in Shandlin Vandervere, "Life on a Native American Reservation," Medium, May 8, 2020. https://medium.com.
17. Amy Linn, "A Forgotten Health Crisis in Navajo Lands," USC Annenberg, July 24, 2018. https://centerforhealthjournalism.org.
18. Quoted in Vandervere, "Life on a Native American Reservation."
19. Quoted in Navajo Nation, "President Nez Meets with the White House's Top Infrastructure Official," February 11, 2022. www.navajo-nsn.gov.
20. Quoted in Frank Vaisvilas, "Land Is Life: How the Oneida Nation Is Reclaiming Its Land, and Its Identity," *Green Bay (WI) Press-Gazette*, August 24, 2020. www.greenbaypressgazette.com.
21. Quoted in Vandervere, "Life on a Native American Reservation."

Chapter Three: Reclaiming Identity

22. Quoted in Tomás Almaguer, *Racial Fault Lines*. Berkeley: University of California Press, 2008, p. 119.
23. Quoted in Marnette Federis and Mina Kim, "Examining the Painful Legacy of Native American Boarding Schools in the US," KQED, August 3, 2021. www.kqed.org.
24. Quoted in Federis and Kim, "Examining the Painful Legacy of Native American Boarding Schools in the US."
25. Dunbar-Ortiz, *The Indigenous Peoples' History of the United States*, p. 151.
26. Quoted in Mary Pember, "'Decolonise and Re-Indigenise': The Ojibwe Language Warrior," Al Jazeera, December 19, 2019. www.aljazeera.com.
27. Quoted in Pember, "'Decolonise and Re-Indigenise.'"
28. Quoted in Dan Ninham, "Anton Treuer: Keeping the Ojibwe Language Alive," Indian Country Today, February 14, 2022. https://indiancountrytoday.com.
29. Anton Treuer, *The Language Warrior's Manifesto: How to Keep Our Languages Alive No Matter the Odds*. St. Paul: Minnesota Historical Society, 2020, pp. 10–11.

Chapter Four: Striving for Rights

30. Quoted in Ray John de Aragón, *New Mexico's Stolen Lands: A History of Racism, Fraud & Deceit*. Charleston, SC: History Press, 2020, p. 94.
31. Max Nesterak, "Uprooted: The 1950s Plan to Erase Indian Country," APM Reports, November 1, 2019. www.apmreports.org.
32. Stephen L. Pevar, *The Rights of Indians and Tribes*. Carbondale: Southern Illinois University Press, 2002, p. 68.

33. Quoted in Nesterak, "Uprooted."
34. Quoted in Peniel E. Joseph, "50 Years Ago Stokely Carmichael Called for 'Black Power,' Galvanizing a Movement," The Root, June 19, 2016. www.theroot.com.
35. Paul Chaat Smith and Robert Allen Warrior, *Like a Hurricane: The Indian Movement from Alcatraz to Wounded Knee.* New York: New Press, 1996, p. 128.
36. Quoted in Nesterak, "Uprooted."
37. Smith and Warrior, *Like a Hurricane,* p. 21.
38. Smith and Warrior, *Like a Hurricane,* p. 110.
39. Dean Chavers, "Alcatraz Occupation Four Decades Ago Led to Many Benefits for American Indians," Indian Country Today, September 13, 2018. https://indiancountrytoday.com.
40. Quoted in Cecily Hilleary, "Native Americans Most at Risk from Impact of Climate Change," VOA, April 19, 2017. www.voanews.com.
41. Quoted in Tara Houska, "Native American Youth to Obama: 'Rezpect' Our Water," Indian Country Today, August 11, 2016. https://indiancountrymedianetwork.com.

Chapter Five: Confronting Challenges

42. Quoted in Jackie Powder, "Healing Historical Trauma," *Johns Hopkins Magazine*, April 15, 2022. https://magazine.jhsph.edu.
43. Maria Yellow Horse Brave Heart, "The American Indian Holocaust: Healing Historical Unresolved Grief," National Institutes of Health, 1998. https://pubmed.ncbi.nlm.nih.gov.
44. Quoted in Powder, "Healing Historical Trauma."
45. Quoted in Culture Forward, "Introduction," Center for American Indian Health, 2022. https://caih.jhu.edu.
46. Mary Koithan and Cynthia Farrell, "Indigenous Native American Healing Traditions," National Institutes of Health, June 1, 2010. www.ncbi.nlm.nih.gov.
47. Quoted in Nicola Jones, "How Native Tribes Are Taking the Lead on Planning for Climate Change," Yale Environment 360, February 11, 2020. https://e360.yale.edu.
48. Quoted in Jones, "How Native Tribes Are Taking the Lead on Planning for Climate Change."
49. Marcello Maviglia, "Healing Historical Trauma Through Ecological Activism and Cultural Practices," Psychiatry Online, April 4, 2017. www.psychiatryonline.it.

FOR FURTHER RESEARCH

Books

Roxanne Dunbar-Ortiz, *The Indigenous Peoples' History of the United States*. Boston: Beacon, 2015.

Kathy Eckles Hooker, *Voices of Navajo Mothers and Daughters: Portraits of Beauty*. Flagstaff, AZ: Soulstice, 2022.

Robin Wall Kimmerer and Monique Gray Smith, *Braiding Sweetgrass for Young Adults: Indigenous Wisdom, Scientific Knowledge, and the Teachings of Plants*. Minneapolis: Zest, 2022.

Antoine Mountain, *Child of Morning Star: Embers of an Ancient Dawn*. Baltimore: Uproot, 2022.

Anton Treuer, *The Language Warrior's Manifesto: How to Keep Our Languages Alive No Matter the Odds*. St. Paul: Minnesota Historical Society, 2020.

Internet Sources

Kevin Gover, "Five Myths About American Indians," *Washington Post*, November 22, 2017. www.washingtonpost.com.

Nicola Jones, "How Native Tribes Are Taking the Lead on Planning for Climate Change," Yale Environment 360, February 11, 2020. https://e360.yale.edu.

Thomas Morton, "Thomas Morton: Manners and Customs of the Indians (of New England), 1637," Fordham University, January 20, 2021. https://sourcebooks.fordham.edu.

Max Nesterak, "Uprooted: The 1950s Plan to Erase Indian Country," APM Reports, November 1, 2019. www.apmreports.org.

Dan Ninham, "Anton Treuer: Keeping the Ojibwe Language Alive," Indian Country Today, February 14, 2022. https://indiancountrytoday.com.

Shandlin Vandervere, "Life on a Native American Reservation," Medium, May 8, 2020. https://medium.com.

Websites

Center for American Indian Health
https://caih.jhu.edu
This organization founded in 1991 runs public health interventions for Native Americans based on traditional culture and spirituality. Programs in-

clude youth suicide prevention, environmental health, and alcohol and drug abuse counseling.

Indian Country Today
https://indiancountrytoday.com
This digital indigenous news source provides comprehensive coverage of Native American current events, issues, culture, history, and lifestyle.

Indigenous Environmental Network
www.ienearth.org
This grassroots network works with indigenous communities and tribal governments to protect sacred sites, land, water, air, and natural resources. The group holds demonstrations, publishes environmental reports, and creates podcasts and other media to organize against climate change.

Native Knowledge 360°
https://americanindian.si.edu/nk360
This program by the National Museum of the American Indian connects students to the contributions of Native Americans in the past and in the present. Educational resources include indigenous contribution to art, technology, geography, history, and numerous other topics.

Radio Free Alcatraz
https://americanarchive.org/catalog/cpb-aacip_28-q23qv3cj2p
Digital archives of the radio shows hosted by Sioux activist John Trudell that were broadcast from Alcatraz Island during the Native American occupation in 1969 and 1970.

Running Strong for American Indian Youth
https://indianyouth.org
This organization is dedicated to creating the next generation of Native American leaders by providing programs that support youth, preserve language and culture, and promote education.

Tribes & Climate Change Program
http://www7.nau.edu/itep/main/tcc
Tribes & Climate Change provides support to Native American nations working to restore the environment and fight climate change. The website provides fact sheets, tribal information, newsletters, and a tool kit for adapting to climate change.

INDEX

Note: Boldface page numbers indicate illustrations.

age of discovery, 10
Aguonia, Jake, 11
Alcantara, Pedro, 29
Alcatraz Island occupation (1969–1971), 42–44
Algonquian language, 13
Allard, LaDonna Brave Bull, 46
American History: A Survey (textbook), 10
American Indian Movement (AIM), 42, 45
American Indian Religious Freedom Act (1978), 37, 44
Apache Nation, 14
arts, 8, 35
   of Southwestern clans, 14–15

Banai, Eddie Benton, 42
Banks, Dennis, 42
Bannock Nation, 14
beavers, **55**, 55–56
Bellecourt, Clyde, 42
Biden, Joe, 7, 27–28
Black Elk (Oglala Lakota elder), 19
Blackfoot people, 13
Black Power movement, 41
boarding schools, 30–33
   historical trauma from, 48
   investigation into, 32
   Native American children in, **31**
Bosque Redondo (reservation), 24–25
Brave Heart, Maria Yellow Horse, 48, 49
Bureau of Indian Affairs (BIA), 32

Campbell, Ben Nighthorse, 38, **39**
Carmichael, Stokely, 41
Carter, Jimmy, 37
Cayuga people, 11, 16
Center for American Indian Health (CAIH), 52, 60–61
Centers for Disease Control and Prevention, 49
Charger, Jasilyn, 7–8, 47
Charles-Newton, Eugenia, 54
Chavers, Dean, 45
Cherokee Nation Businesses (CNB), 23–24
Cherokee Nation Film Office, 24
Cherokee Phoenix (newspaper), 20
Cherokee (Tsalagi) Nation, 7
   develops written language, 20
   forced relocation of, 21–22
   rebuilding of, 22–23
Cheyenne Nation, 13, 17, 19
Chickasaw Nation, 20, 21
Child Welfare Act (1978), 32–33
Choctaw Nation, 20, 21
   forced relocation of, **25**
clans, 11
climate change, 54–56
Constitution, US, 16
Cooley, Nikki, 54
Creek Nation, 20, 21
cultural regions, **12**
Culture Forward program, 52
Curtis Act (1898), 23

Dakota Access Pipeline (DAPL) protests, **46**, 46–47
Day, Charlotte, 41, 42
Day, Clyde, 41
Day, Dorene, 42
Deganawida (Iroquois elder), 16
Department of Interior, US, 32
Department of Justice, US, 50
A Description of New England (Smith), 13
Diné Nation. *See* Navajo Nation
domestic violence, 48, 50–51, 54
Dunbar-Ortiz, Roxanne, 13–14, 31–32

environmental justice activism, 45–47

Farrell, Cynthia, 53
Five Civilized Tribes (Cherokee, Chickasaw, Choctaw, Creek, and Seminole), 20
Franklin, Benjamin, 16

gaming operations, 9, 23
Garcia, Anthony, 42–43
Gathering of Nations (Albuquerque), 37
Gibson, Jeffrey, 35
Goldtooth, Dallas, 46
Goldtooth, Tom, 45–46
Gover, Kevin, 6
The Grandfathers Speak (Hitakonanu'laxk), 18
Grass Dance Society, 35
Great Law of Peace, 16
Great Spirit, 15–16

Haaland, Deb, 7, 32, 52
Harjo, Sterlin, 7
Haudenosaunee Confederacy (Six Nations of the Iroquois), 11–12, 16, 26
Hill, Carrie, 35
historical trauma, 48–49
   ongoing effects of, 51
Hitakonanu'laxk (Lenapé chief), 18
Hohokam people, 10
Hopi people, 9
Hoskin, Chuck, Jr., 24

Indian country, 7
Indian Country Today (website), 61
Indian Education Act (1972), 44
Indian Gaming Regulatory Act (1988), 23
Indian Relocation Act (1956), 40–41
Indian Self-Determination and Education Assistance Act (1975), 44

Indians of All Tribes (IOAT), 43
Indian Termination Act (1953), 38–40, 45
Indian Territory (Oklahoma), 21
Indigenous Environmental Network, 45, 61
Iroquois clans. *See* Haudenosaunee Confederacy
Iroquois False Face Society, 35

Jackson, Andrew, 21

Karuk people, 10
Kiowa Nation, 13
Koithan, Mary, 53
Kowa people, 9

Lakota Nation, 13
language(s), 10, 11
    written Cherokee, 20
The League of the Ho-dé-no-sau-nee or Iroquois (Morgan), 16
Lenapé people, 13, 18
life expectancy, **5**
Little Earth housing project (Minneapolis), 45
Longest Walk (1978), 45
Long Walk, 24–25

Madison, James, 16
Malatre, Clovia, 40–41
Martin, Robert, 8
Martinez, Xiuhtezcatl, 7–8
Mashpee people, 13
Maviglia, Marcello, 56
missing and murdered indigenous peoples (MMIP) movement, 54
Mitchell, George, 42
Mohawk people, 9, 11, 16
Mono people, 10
Montgomery, Lindsay, 30
Mooney, James, 22
Morgan, Lewis Henry, 16
Morton, Thomas, 18
Mosay, Archie, 33

Nantucket people, 13
National Survey on Drug Use and Health, 49
Native American nations
    cultural regions of, **12**
    of Great Plains/Pacific Northwest, 13–14
    of Southwest, 14–15, 29
    warfare between, 17
Native Americans
    campaigns to exterminate, 8
    demographics of, **4–5**
    numbers living in Indian country, 7
    numbers of Americans identifying as, 6
    pre-fifteenth century population size, 10
    stereotypes of, 6
Native Knowledge 360°, 61
Navajo (Diné) Nation, **5**, 7, 9, 14, **27**
    conditions on reservation, 26–28
    current conditions of, 26–28
    Long Walk of, 24–25
Nesterak, Max, 38
Nez, Jonathan, 27–28
Nixon, Richard, 45

Obama, Barack, 47
Ojibwa Nation, 13
Ojibwa people, 13
Ojibway, Joseph, 49
Oklahoma, 23
Oneida people, 11, 16, 26
    buy back of ancestral lands by, 28
Onondaga people, 11, 16
Oshkaabewis Native Journal, 34

Paiute Nation, 14
Patuxet people, 13
Pawnee Nation, 13
Pevar, Stephen L., 40
post-traumatic stress disorder (PTSD), 51
powwows, 35–37, **36**
Pratt, Richard Henry, 30
Pueblo Nation, 14

Radio Free Alcatraz, 61
Radio Free Alcatraz (radio program), 43–44
Reservation Dogs (TV program), 8, **8**, 24
Running Strong for American Indian Youth, 61

salmon, **53**, 55–56
Seminole Nation, 20, 21
Seneca people, 11, 16
Sherman, William T., 8
Sherman Institute, 30
Shoshone Nation, 14
Sioux Wars, **17**, 19
Six Nations of the Iroquois. *See* Haudenosaunee Confederacy
smallpox, 17, 18
Smith, Jaune Quick-to-See, 8
Smith, John, 13
Smith, Paul Chaat, 42, 44
spirituality, 15–16, 22, 28, 29
    ancestral lands and, 47
    links to natural world, 52–53
    powwows and, 36–37
stereotypes, 6
substance abuse, 9, 51, 52
suicide, 31, 32, 49–50
Swinomish Nation, 54–55

Tocqueville, Alexis de, 21
Trail of Tears, 21–22, **25**
Treaty of Fort Laramie (1868), 43
Treuer, Anton, 33–34, 37
tribal nations, 6–7
Tribes & Climate Change Program, 61
Trudell, John, 43–44
Tsalagi Nation. *See* Cherokee Nation
Tulalip Tribes, 55
Turner, Dennis, 42–43
turquoise, 15
Tuscarora people, 11

Ute Nation, 14

Van Buren, Martin, 22

Wampanoag tribal confederation, 13
Warrior, Robert Allen, 42, 44
Watt, Marie, 8
Webster, Bobbi, 26, 28
Whitbeck, Les B., 51
Williams, Joseph, 55
Wounded Knee (SD), 19

Yupik people, 16, 53
Yurok people, 10

PICTURE CREDITS

Cover: Shutterstock.com

4: aelitta/iStock (top)
4: AJ_Watt/iStock (middle)
4: Maury Aaseng (map)
5: grandriver/Shutterstock.com (top)
5: Maxim Studio/Shutterstock (flag)
5: Maury Aaseng (pie and bar charts)
5: montes-Bradley/iStock (bottom left)
8: TCD/Prod.DB/Alamy Stock Photo
12: Maury Aaseng
15: Francesco Abrignani/Alamy Stock Photo
17: akg-images/Newscom
21: Historic Images/Alamy Stock Photo
25: Picture History/Newscom
27: Arterra Picture Library/Alamy Stock Photo
31: Everett Collection/Bridgeman Images
34: Associated Press
36: Pierre-Jean DURIEU/Alamy Stock Photo
39: Newscom
43: Bob Kreisel/Alamy Stock Photo
46: Pacific Press Production Corp./Alamy Stock Photo
50: Heritage Image Partnership Ltd/Alamy Stock Photo
53: Design Pics Inc/Alamy Stock Photo
55: Ian Dewar/Alamy Stock Photo

Sources: Native Americans by the Numbers
- Nicholas Jones, et al., "2020 Census Illuminates Racial and Ethnic Composition of the Country," US Census Bureau, August 12, 2021. www.census.gov.
- "Profile: American Indian/Alaska Native," U.S. Department of Health and Human Services Office of Minority Health, January 11, 2022.
- Associated Press, "Navajo Nation Tops Cherokee to Become Largest Tribe in US," Voice of America, May 19, 2021. www.voanews.com."Profile: American Indian/Alaska Native."
- Simon Romero, "Navajo Nation Becomes Largest Tribe in U.S. After Pandemic Enrollment Surge," *New York Times*, May 21, 2021.
- Amber Pariona, "Biggest Indian Reservations in the United States," WorldAtlas, June 5, 2018. www.worldatlas.com.
- "Profile: American Indian/Alaska Native."
- "Profile: American Indian/Alaska Native."

**Marion Public Library
1101 6th Ave
Marion, IA 52302
(319) 377-3412**